WHAT A DIFFERENCE A DAY MAKES

A Survival Guide for Women

Kerri Cartelli

PublishAmerica
Baltimore

ISBN: 1-4241-4556-2
PUBLISHED BY PUBLISHAMERICA, LLLP
www.publishamerica.com
Baltimore

Printed in the United States of America

Dedication

This book is dedicated to my husband Domenic and my three children, Domenic, Anna and Charlotte. They have taught me many lessons that I have and will carry with me forever. Domenic is my rock and my children are my life.

Disclaimer

The advice contained in this material may not be suitable for everyone. The author devised the information to present her opinion about the subject matter. The author obtained the information contained in this book from her own personal experience. Nor does she imply or intend any guarantees. Should the reader need psychological or marital advice, he or she must seek services from a competent professional. The author also disclaims any liability, from loss or risk taken by individuals who directly or indirectly act on the information contained in this book. The author believes the advice she's presented here is sound, but readers cannot hold her responsible for either the actions they take or the result of those actions.

Table of Contents

Introduction

When you open yourself up to other women
and a Circle of Sisterhood, a new world presents itself.
Would you like to be emotionally happy?
Would you like to be emotionally happy as soon as possible?

Well then hold on to your boot straps, because you are about to go on the ride of your life. If you remain open and willing to do what it takes, then you are on your way to a life free from emotional detention, a life beyond your wildest dreams.

My name is Kerri Cartelli. I am a wife, mother, teacher, sister, daughter, aunt, friend and woman. Empowerment is a fundamental necessity in my life. Loving my family is imperative, but loving myself is essential.

My life has taken me down different paths. The system I an introducing in this book is a cultivation of all of my experiences. These tools are what I use and have used on a daily basis throughout my life and struggles. These tools have enabled me to live a life beyond my wildest dreams. I know that if you follow these principles and put them into motion in your own life, that you can and will reap the same emotional rewards that I have. I am sure that no matter where you are in your life, that this system can help you reach anything you set your mind to.

My system is for anyone who wants to live a balanced and peaceful life. You will learn how to live every day to the fullest through letting go of everyday issues that cloud your life. You will be pleasantly surprised to know that this system is so easy, it is almost laughable. As you go through the process, you'll wonder why you never thought of it yourself. But, that is just it! We don't think of these things on our own. We need each other!!!!

Let me begin by saying that life does not have to be a struggle. As human beings, it is our nature to constantly second guess ourselves. Letting go of sadness, pain, self doubt, low self esteem and learning how to laugh at ourselves and have fun is the key to a positive and empowering life. Feelings of anger from childhood, resentment towards our parents, fear of intimacy and the "not good enough" syndrome lead us to misunderstand our current state of emotion.

Everything that happens, and has happened in our lives effect us today. Looking in mirrors and sizing ourselves up constantly, eventually drains us of our love for living, laughing and sharing. Utilize your sense of inner knowing and tap into a place that has probably been lost for some time. Through my system, you can create a cycle of learning by being real, mirroring the best in others, inviting emotional safety into your life, and letting go of perfection

Sharing ourselves with our spouses, children, mothers, fathers, sisters, brothers, etc. is what we begin to lose as we go deeper into our dented subconscious. I say dented because through these principles, you can bang out those dents and be almost as good as new.

When was the last time you walked out of the kitchen, turned on the radio and started singing as loud as you could? Danced a silly dance, or just laughed a deep down in your belly, tear jerking laugh?

Have you watched your little one lately? Watch what they do when you turn on that music and copy them. You'll be pleasantly surprised how good you feel.

Being able to let go is not something that most people understand.

As it goes, many of us in this society have learned how to internalize or "stuff" our emotions. Not many people have the gift of communicating effectively in their relationships.

There are two critical aspects of "letting go" and creating positive relationships.

The first is becoming a more expressive verbalizer of what your thoughts and feelings are. The second is becoming a more effective and active listener of what is being said to you.

Becoming a more expressive verbalizer is a difficult task. People are trained to either say exactly what they are thinking the moment they think it, or, to not say anything at all. There is something called being "brutally" honest and the other is being a doormat.

As children in school, we learn to raise our hands if we have a question or answer, but if those questions or answers are not correct, we are shot down and made to feel "stupid." So, in retrospect, we are taught to have all the answers or don't ask any questions as we might be wrong.

These roots that have been planted, in which we grow from, are the very roots that create the person we've become. All of our experiences in life and processes of dealing with life have made us what we are today. Are you happy with the person you've become? Can you truly say that you are able to handle any problem that you encounter?

As women, we often hold our tongues in the fear that we may not know what we are talking about. Or on the other hand, we have "diarrhea of the mouth." Women are seen as gossipers who thrive on the misfortune of other women. We are seen as complainers, whiners and/or naggers.

*****

How do you see yourself in terms
of verbalizing with others?

*****

The biggest lesson I've learned in life is to THINK before I speak. When faced with a possible confrontation with someone, I will think through what I am going to say to them first. I will not just react. That is a big no, no. When you come from a place of authenticity and honesty, you can never go wrong in a relationship.

Becoming a more effective and active listener is even harder then the latter. It is so much easier to counsel than to be counseled, to react than to resist and to judge rather than be judged. Listening is a gift. To listen effectively in an honest relationship is the best gift we can give to each other. As children, we are constantly looking for attention. We are "attention addicts." Any way I could get attention was the way for me. For example, when a child is listening to a story being read, how many times do they raise their hands to explain what is going on and how it relates to their lives? Rather than listening to the story, they feel the need to tell the reader every experience they've had that is similar to the story. I see this in adults all the time.

Pay attention the next time you are on the telephone with a loved one or friend. Are you really listening to what they are saying or are you thinking of every way it relates to you. If we can take a little bit of everything we hear from others and put it to work in our lives, we are able to open our minds to other ideas.

There are many opportunities that present themselves to us on a daily basis. I believe that the answers to all of my questions come through people. Many times, the answers come from people I would least expect to have the answers.

One needs to be able to interpret and understand the message in the "here and now" without allowing preconceived notions to filter and distort the intentions of the person you are communicating with.

#1

Establish a Sisterline

This is one of, if not the most, important principles in my system. Although it may seem to be the easiest, you will find that it is difficult to do. Every morning, no matter what is going on in my home, life or relationship with my husband, I get on that telephone. They are a network of women that I have at my disposal to speak to relating to anything going on in my life.

The key is to surround yourself with positive women. Now I know that everyone in your "secret circle" is not always positive, but that is the beauty of having a network of women. Not just one "best friend" to confide in and get support from. I call it the "secret circle" because this group of women does not have to know each other, be friends with each other, or even have anything in common. In fact, it is better if the latter is the case. Then, you never have to be concerned with anyone "talking about" what you are saying.

The other aspect of the network is unconditional support. When two people have a foundation of support in which they are always on the same page, the support is unconditional. You are there for each other without the ties of outside issues or other individuals.

When my 5 year old daughter was diagnosed with a seizure disorder two years ago, the first thing I thought of was, "How could this be happening to me?" Me? Was it happening to me? No!!!!! It was and is happening to her! She's the one who has to go through the seizures and recover. She's the one who has to take medication twice a day. She's the one who has to live with the effects in her brain. Yes! She's the one. Not me. But, why is my first reaction to play the victim. I personally think it is because we normally go there. We've been so brainwashed to be weak and powerless. So, what did I do? I called my women!!! I'll say it again. I called my women. And guess what happened? I got through it being able to support my daughter and genuinely help her function in her power. Even my 5 year old daughter is powerful. Her power is within her! It is within you and in your secret circle. Tap into it!! Don't be afraid. You'll feel a freedom you never felt before.

In early Native American culture, the woman in the tribe was revered as a life giving force. They were mother earth.

They were the nourishers of life. Being good mothers and raising healthy families was the most important achievement. They were healers and storytellers. In some tribes, when a woman had a baby "her women" would surround her and make sure she was safe and taken care of. Women were strong. They were empowered. They were not victims. They didn't have that choice. We are strong women. We are not victims of our lives and we DO have choices.

*****

Stand up, place your hand on your heart and make a declaration!
I AM RESPONSIBLE FOR 100% OF MY LIFE!!!!!!!

*****

The power within you is entirely defined by the power you give back. The only way we can succeed in life is by giving back to others. The wonderful thing about speaking to a woman every day is that you give back to her. How many of you have ever called a friend and at the end of the conversation she tells you how much you've helped her. What? I've helped you? You can't believe it! That is the power of putting yourself out there. Getting out of your comfort zone! We'll talk more about that later.

When I was in my early twenties, I didn't like women. I saw women as the competition. Any man I was involved with was literally taken hostage by me and doom to a period of he said/she said. Jealous! Boy was I jealous. The problem wasn't the boyfriend, it was the woman he might have glanced at on the street, or the cashier he said "thank you" to a little too nicely for my liking. Anything that happened in terms of other women made me go into competition mode. Why didn't he like me? What about her is better than me? Blah, blah, blah..........

What I learned, at the cost of some good relationships, was that I didn't know how to relate to other women. That was the problem. It wasn't anyone else but me not being able to see the beauty in others. I was always focusing on me.

This network you create for yourself will force you to learn how to confide and relate to women in a way that will empower your soul. It will force the power within you to burst out and help many, many others in your life.

*****

Here are two things that you will do everyday to build a network of sisters or a "secret circle" for unconditional support.

First, make a list of all of the women you know in your life that are positive. (Not the ones that constantly complain.)

Second, for 90 days I want you to call one of the women on your list everyday so that you can establish a sisterline.

A network of women that you can identify with, confide in, bounce ideas off of, etc.

It will change your life.

#2

Journaling for Sanity

When many of us were little girl's, we bought or were given little diaries with keys. We would write all of our thoughts and dreams. The boys we liked. Why I was angry at mom, etc. Then, one day, someone (usually a little brother or sister) finds the diary. We are mortified. We are embarrassed. We are taught a lesson that will stay with us for the rest of our lives. Lesson #1: don't trust anyone. Lesson #2: keep your innermost thought inside (stuff it) rather than write them down.

Although this little scenario is a little indulged, you get my point. We are taught as young girls to keep our feelings and negative emotions inside. Do not voice them or you will be frowned upon. If you do voice your controversial opinions you are a big mouth!

The problem is that once we get to young adulthood, the gift that we were given as young girls through writing is gone. Writing or journaling is unsurpassed in its benefits to the female (or male) psyche. Venting, in a safe environment, is the healthiest way to deal with emotional issues. Many people use different forums to vent. Play some music; some do sports, some go to psychotherapy and some journal. There's a wonderful feeling attached to a beautiful little book tucked away in a night drawer that is yours and yours alone.

The only barrier that many people are confronted with is, "what do I write about."

The most prevalent reason I've heard people say that they don't journal is because they don't know what to write about, or they don't even know where to begin. The beauty of journaling is that it is completely yours. You don't have to be right, or worry about being judged or criticized. Whatever you write is for your eyes only.

There is a lot to be said about writing. When you put your thoughts on paper, it is a great asset. You can see how what you're thinking about actually sounds. Many times, when we are very emotional, we are not very rational. When we run with emotion, we can often ruin or damage relationships and trusts. This is unnecessary. When we read how we are feeling, it's there in black and white. You give yourself time to cool off or grieve, etc. The greatest part about keeping a journal is that when you are feeling better, you can go back and look at what you had written. Often times, I will look back at a journal and find myself giggling.

Whether you decide to share your writing with someone is your choice. And what a wonderful thing that would be to feel comfortable enough with another woman to be able to share your inner most thoughts and feelings with another human being. Imagine how you can help someone else! Remember, it is all about who we affect in life. We leave a legacy for those in our lives that will carry on after we've gone. What legacy will you leave? How do you want your daughters to live their lives? They're watching us!

If you decide to take my advice, which is part of the system, the following will be extremely helpful to get you started.

Here are a few guidelines for getting started:

- Work in a quiet place.
- Find a daily retreat and explore the power of writing in your life.
- Who are you?
- What is your background?
- What experiences have brought you to this time and place in your life?
- What life changing mistakes have you made that you haven't dealt with?
- What successes have you experienced in your life?
- What are you grateful for?
- What do you actually want?

One of the greatest feeling of satisfaction is when a woman shops. Don't get me wrong, I am not saying all women are shopaholics, I am just saying it feels good to buy things we like. Anyway, buying your journal is a great thing. Spend some time finding a journal that will beckon you to open it. Whether it is expensive or thrifty. Make it yours! Paste pictures of your kids on it! Anything that will make it inviting.

Now, write, write and write some more!!!! I suggest writing whenever the mood hits you. Use your journal as a tool to make it through the day. A great time to journal is anytime. When you're happy, angry, sad, lonely, tired, sick or excited, you should write. Once you have a pretty good track record of writing for a week or two or three, go back and read what you've written. Look at the growth throughout this time. Or, look at what hasn't changed. Where can you make changes to become the empowered woman you want to be.

*****

Stand up, place your hand on your heart and make a declaration. Yell it!

"I HAVE THE POWER TO BE THE WOMAN I WANT TO BE!"

*****

Now that you've taken the first step, continue to discover your power within through these simple steps. You can do it! Have faith in yourself.

#3

Jumping for Joyfulness

Think of a time when you woke up in the morning, got up out of bed, looked back at your pillow and wished that you could stay there. What is different about today from yesterday when you woke up and felt fantastic? Are you sick? Are you in another time and space? No! You are human. What next? You think to yourself, "My day is ruined."

Guess what? You're day is not ruined because you know exactly what to do to change it.

Now, I am a mommy. I have three children who are under the age of 6. What do you think they love to do? DANCE!!!!! A great way, and the perfect tool to "get out of you", is to move that body!!!!

So many of us are stagnant and stationary! The last time you jumped or danced or sang was probably at your wedding. Anyway, get up, go into the living room, turn on the music and dance your blues away. Look at your little one. As I stated earlier, watch closely what they do. Clear your mind of the nonsense of the day. Whatever you have to do can wait. Even your phone call to your "sister!" Shake that coolly. Wave those arms. Get some air between your feet and the floor. In other words, MOVE YOUR BODY. Once you get the hang of this, it will become something you'll want to make a daily or weekly ritual.

*****

Stand up, place your hand on your heart and make a declaration. Say it loud and smile!

I WILL RESTART MY DAY TO FULFILL MY DREAMS.

*****

The worst thing that can happen to us is to get "stuck" in a moment and let it ruin the day. It's like the domino effect. The scenario unfolds and we grab on to it and run. Sometimes, it is more comfortable for us to feel badly than to do a little work to get out of it and feel better. For those of you who have negative past experiences, it is even easier to hold on to the bad feeling. You want to know why? Because we're used to feeling badly! There is more comfort in familiar feelings than in change. If my mind tends to go to the negative, it is hard for me to do the few things it takes to feel better. That is not comfortable. We'll get more into that later.

As a woman and a mother, I know that the most frustrating aspect of my life is lack of control. I find that I lash out at the people that are closest to me. My children are with me constantly and boy, can they push my buttons. It amazes me at how frustrated I can get at a three year old child. This is when these techniques really come in handy.

So, you're in the grocery store, the day is going great, and your little one decides to have a holy fit. Surprise!!! Isn't it amazing how quickly a great day can turn into a nightmare? One technique I've found that works wonders in this situation is to stop, close your eyes, plant your feet in place, arm to sides, head up tall reaching the sky and now…….BREATH! Once you take that breath, you will feel your body grow an inch taller. That feeling in the pit of your stomach will fade and your little wonders screams will not seem so loud. Those women who are staring at you shaking their heads will disappear and most important of all, your day will go on as if nothing had happened. Bliss! Bliss! Bliss! Until the next tantrum. Just remember, practice makes perfect.

Try this exercise:

*****

Stand up, close your eyes, plant your feet in place.

Arm to sides, head up tall reaching the sky and
now........BREATH!
In through your nose and out through your mouth.
Fill up your belly and release.
Be aware of your body.
Feel it growing and getting stronger with every breath.

*****

You did it! Be proud of yourself. Look at yourself in the mirror and say, "I can do this!" Remember, when you change one thing about your day, it will change.

#4

Meditate for Wisdom

Now, I know what you're thinking. No one really thinks they have time for meditating. Remember, meditation is what you make of it. My idea of meditation, and I can only share my experience, is sitting still and being within my power. Clearing my mind and trying not to think. It is listening and taking in all that is around you.

I've stated earlier that I am a mother of three. Throughout the day I am doing my different things. As many of you are mothers, we all know that we wear many hats throughout the day. Cleaning, driving, cooking, cleaning some more, etc. You get the point. I very rarely wear my "play with my kids" hat. Not intentionally, but during the day, time just evaporates and all of the sudden it is bedtime.

So, the other day, my two girls are on the trampoline. I go out there to make sure they are okay and I decide to climb in. My intention was to be the watch dog, not to bounce. What do you know! I bounced, and I bounced and I bounced. Then, I lay down on my back and stared up at the trees and the clouds. We saw dinosaurs and elephants. Before I knew it, it was an hour later and I realized that I had just meditated. It was unintentional and not planned, but it was a wonderful release. I felt a weight lift off my shoulders and continued my day with a different feeling.

For those of you who are so jammed up that even laying still for a moment makes you nervous, you need this more that anyone. The time factor is another reason why many people cannot meditate. I look at meditation as just a time to sit still and clear up. When I think of a free thinking moment, or non-thinking moment, I think of driving. A good percent of the time we are sitting at traffic lights, waiting for school buses, sitting in children's bedrooms with an aversion to sleep, taking showers or baths (if we're lucky) etc. The list goes on.

There are many different things we can do to "meditate." Just taking the time out to relax. By relax, I mean sit still! I know that sitting still for me used to immediately prompt my body to go into sleep mode. If I sat for more than 5 minutes throughout my hectic day, I felt like sleeping. But as with any habit, once your body becomes accustomed to relaxing at one or more points during the day, you will be able to do so and come out feeling rested and ready to continue your daily tasks. Now I know you're all thinking, "She's crazy. When am I gonna do that?" Just remember that I've been where you are and I know how you feel. All I know is that when I'm calmer, everybody else around me seems calmer. Try some of these ideas for relaxing.

• Keep a good book available for you to sit and read. If you have children, let them pick a book and at a designated time, set your timer for 20 minutes and everyone curl up and read.

• Lie down and listen to soothing music. Again, set your timer for 20 minutes and just listen.

• Take a leisurely walk. Now, I don't mean to put on your ankle weights and go power walking. I mean leisurely. Look at the foliage. Find some caterpillars or collect leaves. Take your time!

• Sit in the tub. If you have a very little one, get in there with her/him. Put bubbles in it and just enjoy life and the life you've created. This will give you a feeling of empowerment beyond words.

• If you have the funds, make an appointment for a facial or massage and go! Many spas offer block discounts. Buy a block and make the appointments ahead of time. If you have a good friend, switch babysitting. You won't believe how good it feels to take care of YOU on a consistent basis.

• Watch a sunrise or sunset. This can be done alone or with others. It's your choice.

The most important thing to do is breath. You wouldn't believe how many people don't breath. I know that when I used to get jammed up, I would notice that I wasn't breathing at all. I was actually holding my breath. A nice long deep in the belly breath can work wonders. Try it and you will see the difference. I promise.

Seize the moment. There are so many missed opportunities to sit still with our minds. Put your thoughts and intentions out to God, Great Spirit, Buddha, Universe or whatever or whomever your Higher Power is at that time. Answers will come to you when you really begin to listen. Talking is over rated. Try it.

*****

Right now, stop what you're doing!
If you want do this with a friend reading it.
Or practice but do it!
Sit down, close your eyes, and clear your mind.
Now.......BREATH!
Take the life giving air in through your nose and out through your mouth.
Be aware of your body. Now, think of that perfect place that you have always dreamed of.
Maybe it's somewhere from childhood that you love to go.
Go there in your mind.
Go and touch something in this wonderful place.
Feel the texture of this place. Smell what is around you.

Taste something. You are there.
Now sit there. Don't let the outside world intrude in this
place. If it does, send it away for the moment.
Keep breathing!
Stay there for as long as you can.
Come back, open your eyes. Feel the calmness about you.
Welcome the real world back and realize how powerful
you are. Carry this with you throughout the day.

*****

YOU JUST MEDITATED!!! AWESOME!
Many people wonder what the benefits of meditation
actually are. Meditation can reduce stress; improve health,
increase awareness, mental clarity and creativity. It is also
instrumental to inner peace, balance and a higher state of
consciousness. Yada, yada, yada! If feels damn good!!!!

If you're really lucky, you can get up early in the
morning. Find a quiet place and relax. Many of you have
heard the saying, "Praying is talking to God and
meditating is listening." Start listening to the things and
people around you. Our minds are so cluttered with
"noise" that we don't hear the important things. When we
really clear our minds, things become a little more
tolerable. They become a little brighter, a little slower and
every time, you will feel a little better about being you.

Everyday my six year old son comes home from
kindergarten. He usually throws his backpack down and

asks me for something. He asks for food, a new toy; go to his friend's house, etc. My first thought and usual reaction is, "can you stop asking me for things. Why are you so ungrateful? Can't you even say hello." Then I turn around and walk away leaving this little boy standing there not knowing what I am talking about because in his mind, all he wanted was to satisfy his basic human needs. Hunger, needs, companionship, etc.

I mention this story because the value of meditation is this. When we clear our minds of the junk that takes up so much space, we then can also focus on our basic human needs. These aren't very difficult to satisfy. Then, like a child, we can create a reality for ourselves based on clarity. I am clear that if I am not hungry or lonely or spiritually unfit, my life will most definitely change for the better. I then become a better mother, sister, daughter, wife, friend, and the list goes on. What a gift!

I can then smile at my baby standing there and say, "I love you, even when you annoy me!"

*****

Stand up, place your hand on your heart and make a declaration. Say it loud.

"I WILL MEDITATE! I WILL MEDITATE! I WILL MEDITATE!"

*****

#5

Declare Your Intentions!

One of the most wonderful things about humans is that we have great power within us. Unfortunately, much of that power is left untapped. Now I'm not talking about being psychic, or seeing dead people, I mean the power of intention. Isn't it true that if you wake up miserable, you can "talk" yourself out of it? Aren't all of the tools in this book teaching us just that? But, that's only if you don't like being miserable. You'd be surprised how many people dig this feeling. Anyway, a declaration is very different than an affirmation. Affirmations are quiet. They're almost like trying to convince yourself that you can do something. You say them to yourself and try to internalize them. A declaration, according to me and my experience, is loud, reverberating and reality. They are truth. Isn't it true we can also talk ourselves into anything? Why not try saying powerful things, for once? They're powerful and empowering and awesome and true. As long as we believe in ourselves. Remember that little train? He knew he could. And he did!

A declaration is something you do so that it vibrates throughout your body. You make it known that you are (insert declaration here).

An intention is something concrete that you would like to become reality.

Did you ever notice that when you want to get someone's attention, be it your spouse, child, employer, etc., they usually don't pay attention. One of the problems I find being a woman is that I tend to seek approval. Therefore, whatever and whenever I say something or tell someone something I've accomplished, I am fishing. We all know what fishing is. It's when we say things out loud hoping for a pat on the back. The day that I didn't have to "fish" anymore was like liberation. To be able to accomplish personal goals or overcome internal and/or external obstacles and not have to tell everyone about it is totally awesome. This is a quiet satisfaction. At first, I was a little anxious. It's almost like a drug. That reaction from others is like a fix. When you don't get it, you don't know what to do with yourself. We're all really like children. When we don't get positive reinforcement we start doing things to get any attention. Why bother doing things that are really cool and not be able to tell anyone. I'll tell you why, because on the day that you can truly be content with yourself and your accomplishments and not have to get reinforcement from others is the day you are free and have found humility.

Listen up ladies (and gentlemen):

- You will never love anyone until you love yourself.
- You will never be able to trust anyone until you trust yourself.
- You will never be able to be absolutely honest with anyone until you are honest within yourself.
- You will absolutely live a good life when you are free of the garbage that has been renting out a room in your head.

Now that you've learned the meaning of life, you are set! Just a little humor to lighten up the mood. Once we can come to an understanding that we are a very little fish in the big pond, we are in good space. I totally love the line from an old movie that says our problems don't amount to a hill of beans in this world. Well said but hard to remember because our hills are always bigger than someone else's. Attention! The earth keeps turning whether we're happy or not. Clocks keep ticking even when we feel like our heads are going to pop off.

Think about a river. Even if there is an obstruction in the river, the water will find another direction to flow. It will keep pushing until it gets through. It just doesn't stop. Although the flow may slow and it may take a little longer to reach its destination, it still gets there. Think of this scenario in your own life. When obstacles come up in life or we get a good dose of Murphy's Law, do you keep forging on, seeking a solution? Or do you stop and sit in the problem? These questions are great to ask yourself. Especially when you're feeling like you're in the problem.

We all pass the dreaded mirror. I don't know any woman who is absolutely happy and content with what they see. If you are one of those women I say "Right on, sister." But, if you're like the old me, you try not to look. The day that I began forcing myself to look in that mirror and say out loud, "You are beautiful!", was the first day I started seeing myself in a new light. The Path of Light and Love. We'll talk more about that later.

When we declare our intentions to the world, we put those words out into the universe. They become real. We hear them and process them. Eventually we believe them. When that happens, we have raised ourselves up a notch on the ladder of life.

*****

Stand up, place your hand on your heart and make a declaration. Say it loud.
"I AM CONFIDENT AND CLEAR. I AM PROUD OF ME!"

*****

Remember, everything we put out there causes a ripple effect. Whatever we jump into create little waves in the lives of those we love and are in relationship with. Do you want those little waves to be positive or negative? You make the choice.

#6

Evicting Your Little Devil

This principle is the one that can make or break your success in any situation be it positive or negative. We all have seen the cartoons with the angel and the devil on the shoulder. One is saying, "Do the right thing" and the other is saying, "be naughty, be very naughty." Well, the tools you will learn in this section are so simple that you may even have fun. How many times have you signed up for a gym membership? You buy the new sneakers, the workout outfit, make up a calendar of days and classes and are all set. Then, the morning you wake up, ready to get in shape, the voices begin. "You don't have to go today. You have so many other things to do. You don't feel good. Where will you bring the kids? You really don't know the ladies in the nursery, blah, blah, blah!" Guess who's talking to you. You got it! Your little devil! Unfortunately most of the time, our little devil is not saying encouraging things. Our little voices are trained to drag us down. To make us re-evaluate a situation and say, Nah. You know who that devil is that says, "You're not that fat, it's the camera!" Take a guess!

Many of you are probably thinking, I don't hear any little voices, what does she think I'm wacko? Well, I am here to tell you that we all HAVE little voices that speak to us. And, without going into the psychological explanation of the subconscious, I will tell you that it is there and it is directly connected to your self esteem. Now, I have no research to back it up. I haven't polled anyone to ask them about their little devil and I haven't been published in any journals of psychology, but what I can say is that it is there and you can EVICT IT! Practice, practice, practice. Isn't that what we teach our kids? Practice makes perfect. The only problem is that you have to first identify it. This is what we will begin to do in the next few minutes.

I want you to think of a time when you were about to do something you really had your heart set on. You had set it up, spent the time and energy into preparation and may have even invested financially in it. Now, like the gym above, you are ready to start and all of a sudden you hear, "Who am I kidding? I can't do that. I'm not good enough. I'm not smart enough. Why try if I'm gonna fail?"

Right at that precise moment I want you to hear the devil's voice. Who does it sound like? Does it sound like that girl in your high school cafeteria. *"Like, you are totally such a loser. You are so fat. You are so uncool, etc."* Or is it the catcher on the baseball team yelling, *"Move in, this won't take long."* We can even name it a cartoon character or someone on television.

Remember, nothing happens immediately. You may be able to identify your devil right away, or it may take some time. For some of us, it is very difficult to actually accept that we may not know everything. That we may be making poor decisions and that we may need help. You've all heard of that river in Egypt. (De-Nile)

So, now we know what we're trying to discover. Now, we have to make an honest effort to identify and accept it. When I say acceptance, I don't mean accept it and not change. I mean accept it and make the decision to change. Throughout your daily routine, pay attention to the small decisions you find yourself making. It's those split second decisions that you have to look out for. The big ones are much easier to mull over and talk over and blah, blah, blah. For example, you're in the car and some guy stops short in front of you. Guess who's there on your shoulder whispering sweet nothings in your ear. Here's your chance. WHO IS IT??????

When you realize who it is you now need to tell it to go away. Don't listen to it. You now know that this devil will keep you blundering down a path of bad decisions and low self esteem. Don't get confused between the devil and your conscience. You conscience let's you know what the right thing to do is. When conscience shows up, you can feel it in your stomach. Tell the devil to go. It's just like hearing someone on the answering machine that you don't want to talk to. Hit delete and let it go. Every time it shows up, hit delete and LET IT GO!

#7

The Discomfort Zone (The Stuffing Factor)

Let me begin this chapter by telling a little story. There was a time in my life when my higher power dropped a huge obstacle in my path. It was a physical, emotional and spiritual obstacle. At times in our lives we always have to change. Whether we want to change or are ready to change, our higher power can make the decision for us and we must oblige.

As many of us do, I was faced with a very busy holiday season (self inflicted). I did everything. Including the food, the gifts, the family, etc. And if that wasn't enough, I decided to have a New Years Eve party. What was I thinking? I'll tell you what I was doing. Not thinking!!!! I lost the focus on myself and dove into people pleasing land. I thought that if I had the perfect Christmas, that my husband wouldn't seem so miserable. I thought that if I had the perfect party, my friends would remember this year for the rest of their lives. We also had a dog that I had decided to give away because he wasn't living up to my unrealistic expectations. That was my breaking point. When I decided to give away the dog, a domino effect began to occur. As a child, there were many times I felt hurt, alone, terrified, lost, abandoned and unwanted. When I decided to give the dog away, I inadvertently began to internalize those feelings and revisited my childhood. That became a problem. Some emotional and mental issues began to surface and I was forced to look at my current life and my past life through a microscope. It was like I was on a stage with everyone watching me and gauging my performance. Sometimes we don't have a choice. We must face our issues and forge ahead.

Well, as always, there was a silver lining. After talking constantly with my therapist, sisters, personal work with my higher power and following my own system, I began to heal and I began to write again. You see, I truly believe that one cannot truly give of themselves if they are not "practicing what they preach". How can I give what I don't have? Once, I discovered that no window is ever truly shut; I decided to start on my path of light and love once more. The truth is that every great challenge in our lives can be seen as a gift. We are given this gift as a sort of rebirth. We are given the opportunity to reinvent ourselves into whatever it is we want to become. A metamorphosis you might say. Mine was one of great change and great freedom. More freedom than I had had before.

Therefore, let's start on the discomfort zone. We cannot change if we are comfortable. We cannot change if we are just tip toeing through the daisies of life. It is imperative that we forge through uncomfortably to grasp the things on the other side. How many times have we discovered that the thing we are most afraid of was actually nothing once we held our breath and went through it?

One thing I know about myself is that when I am very emotional about an issue or something I would like to do, I do not think with my rational mind. It is all emotions. We all know that when we are very emotional it is difficult to see the truth in any situation. We're not using our rational minds. Emotions are not fact and they can change at any time. Now, don't get me wrong. I've started many projects and ran with them purely through emotion and unless I stopped and looked at the situation with intelligence, it usually ended with a different outcome then I had expected. Many times, women will take on projects out of feelings of obligation. We also take on things that appear to be easy. Remember, when you are in the discomfort zone, things are not easy. In the discomfort zone, we take things on that are hard and we do them. We do this because we can grow through the experience and come out of it with more power within. Remember, we are powerful women.

I remember one of the first times I decided to go onstage

and sing in front of an audience. I'm a singer you know. Anyway, I decided to go for it. What a test of courage that was. My belly was doing back flips and my hands were sweating and I had to use the restroom at least a thousand times until it was my turn to get up there. But I have to say. After the first few seconds of total and utter horror, I started to loosen up. I then realized that I kind of liked being up there giving it all I had and doing what I said I was going to do. Now, the comfortable thing would have been to say forget it. I'm not ready. But, the uncomfortable thing to do was to just go for it. And I did. I've been getting up in front of people to sing ever since. I still get a twinge of discomfort every time but that's the great thing about it.

I want you to think about something you've wanted to do for a long time. Is it to join a playgroup with your children or take a class at the community center? Finally join that gym and actually go there and exercise. (That's a whopper!) What is it that is holding you back? What is keeping you from walking through that door or making that phone call? We've all been there. My excuse has always been that I had the kids and nowhere to leave them. I didn't even consider the daycare they provided at the gym itself. When you finally take the baby steps towards a goal, no matter how insignificant, you get a sense of pride that no one can take away.

Have you ever noticed that when you have either a problem or a complaint that you know will not be taken seriously, you suck it up. Or, when someone treats you unfairly or is unkind to you, you suck it up. That's the stuffing factor. We stuff the feelings down so we don't feel them. Why do you think there are so many addicts and alcoholics out there? Booze and drugs are perfect ways to forget about anything. Anyway, the problem with stuffing our emotions is that eventually, they will come out. I personally think that if we learn to truly communicate with others honestly, that we will not stuff. We will give our views and opinions with pride and feel confident in our position. We will not fear what others say and what they think. The people pleasing will end.

It's pretty unknown to many women that there stuffing their feelings on a regular basis can actually make you ill. That feeling in your stomach, or belly barometer, can let you know immediately if you aren't saying what you really want to say. Try to begin recognizing your physical feelings throughout the day. Your body will tell you when you are not feeling or acting or being treated the right way. Once you begin to actually feel your body's signals, you'll know when things just aren't right within yourself. It's so much better to feel good. You'll like it!

*****

Stand up and say;
I cannot change if I am comfortable.
I will push through my fear and conquer anything.

#8

You've Lost That Lovin' Feeling!

So, you wake up one morning and there are kids screaming, clothing strewn all over the room, toys at every footstep, and you think, "When did this happen?" I'll tell you what happened. Life! There are times when I stop and look around me with a husband who works all the time and three small children and think, "How did I get here?" What happened to that young girl full of life always on the go? There are times in my life when it's hard to grasp that what I'm living is actually my life. The life I created for myself willingly. Women tend to start looking for something to fill the void. They feel that an empty space. We just can't understand what that feeling in our stomach. Something's missing. After a long and hard path to learning about myself, I realized what that is. It is me mourning the loss of my youth. The early twenties.

The hardest thing to do is to let go of your young and single persona. That life you had when you were younger is in the past. Now it's time embrace your new married motherhood. It took me a while. It took me three children and staying at home. Why did I keep moving the furniture? The principles I've laid out in this book are the reason I am content with my new life. I say new because the revelation was recent.

People say that being a mother is the hardest job in the world, but I disagree. I think that being a good wife to my husband is the hardest job in the world. Sometimes I think to myself, "When did I become a nanny and a maid." Those are the times when I have to look back and remember what my initial intentions were when I got married. Sometimes we forget why we got married in the first place. I know that I got married to start a family. Yet, when I'm home alone for the third night in a row, eating cookies on the couch and watching reality TV I just can't seem to bring myself back to that place of being grateful.

For me, being a good wife, and when I say good wife, I don't mean standing at the door with slippers and a pipe; I mean being caring and loving to the man I married. It's very easy to lose that feeling. This is the point when I again say to myself, "How did I get here?" One of the things I do is look at old photos. That's the quickest way for me to remember. There was a reason I married this guy.

But, the one single rule I follow to keep my marriage alive is very simple. Are you ready to hear it? I just SHUT UP! You may think this is funny but I sometimes actually tape up a sign on the window above the kitchen sink with these words on it. It is a reminder to keep all of my little opinions to myself. Because newsflash ladies, he can't hear you. Nor does he want to. When I first heard this and realized it to be true I was angry. What do you mean he doesn't want to listen to me? I'm his wife, his woman, his confidant. NOPE!

Now I'm not saying he doesn't love me more than anything and wants to spend the rest of his life with me. I'm saying that all of my daily concerns about who said what to whom and why he or she looked at me that way or they didn't wave when I drove by. That doesn't matter to him. He wants to know that he has underwear in his drawer, food in the fridge and that the television is working. These are very important things to him.

In the first chapter of the book I talked about a Circle of Sisterhood. This is when you need it the most. This is where you vent and talk about all the things that are ailing you. Your women want to know because they are going through the same thing. They feel your pain and anguish. I get excited when I find something on sale; he wants to know why I was out shopping again. My woman wants to know where I got it and when the sale is over. You get it? The only two things my husband wants to do for me is provide shelter and food and have nooky. If he thinks he's failing at either of these tasks he will become defensive. He will feel as if I am attacking his primal manhood. He'll think I hate him.

The only way for me to show my husband that I love him, because men see action and not words, is to SHOW HIM, if you know what I mean. I know you're tired at night when he's in the mood. I know that you'd love to turn over and say, "Tomorrow night, I swear." The message he gets is that he's not doing his job. That he's failed. Then, tomorrow night comes along and you say the same thing. Hey, I totally understand where you're coming from. You want to know why? Because, I AM A WOMAN AND YOUR HUSBAND IS NOT! He will never understand. Even, if he says he does!!!!!!!! Sex is an amazing thing. I know that mothers with small children see it as a blur. We're exhausted, have more weight on us than we'd like and things are sagging every which way. But, believe it or not, most husbands don't see us that way. If we are confident in ourselves and truly love ourselves, they love us too. If I don't ask my husband how I look five times in five minutes he appreciates the independence.

Here's a scenario I want you to consider. It's been a while since you fooled around. I'm saying a month or so. You feel like he's distant. You don't talk that much or hug that much. You are feeling down about yourself because he hasn't been noticing you. So, you practically sterilize the house because you clean it so well. You make sure the kids are all together and calm when he gets home. You make his favorite dinner. The kids are in bed early. That is awesome. Then, at bedtime, he gets in there are rubs you in his special way and you are asleep. Ladies, everything you did that day have just fell out of his brain forever!!!!!!

Now, consider this scenario. Same feelings as before, same situation. But you don't clean the house that day as well. The kids are lunatics as usual and you have him bring home pizza for dinner. At bedtime, when he turns to rub you in his special way, you're bright eyed and bushy tailed and ready to go. SHAZAAM!!!!!!! You've finally figured it out.

Suddenly, the next day you get a phone call from him just to see how you're doing. You might even get an offer to go out and do something for yourself. Maybe he suggests a babysitter so you can spend more time together. He may even turn off the television that night when you get into bed. It's a miracle. You've found the way to a man's heart. Don't believe the food thing, he wants loving. This is the only way, according to me and my experience that he will begin to notice his wife again. Because remember, you are a mother and a wife. Not just a mother. It's very important that you see the difference. What happens to us is that we become mothers and we don't behave like wives anymore. Then, we get angry when they don't notice us.

Some of you may be saying, "She's crazy!" Try it and you'll see. So the gist of this chapter is, shut up and fools around with your man. Your relationship will change. I promise.

decisions based on "Karma". It controls my urges to be the old me. When I do the next right thing, I can never go wrong. There are no thoughts of revenge or resentment. I just know that I have done all I can and give my control back to the spirit. I have something called a belly barometer. That's my conscience. It's exactly like the Golden Rule we all learned in school as children. Everything that happens to us is how you perceive it. When you live your life trying to do the right thing, you can never go wrong.

If you find it difficult to think of someone or something to pray to because of childhood issues, past memories, or just not believing, try this. Clear your mind and look at your children. If you don't have children, look at the beauty around you. Realize that something is out there that created all of these wonderful things. That something that carries you through life's awful moments. That thought that pops into your mind when you are feeling totally lost. You can name this spirit and look to it. This can be your light. It is what it is. It's what you make it. Only you need to believe. This power will carry you and console you and give you power that you will never lose. This is the gift.

#10

The Secret of My Success List

Finally, the time has come for us to see what we have done right and what we could have done differently. So many times we beat ourselves up and view ourselves through the eyes of society, our neighbors and those whose view are clouded. We so seldom give ourselves the credit we deserve. We almost never see the right things. This exercise will help you to see yourself in a new light. It will unburden you and take away the self doubt. At the end of the day I take a piece of paper or my journal and write down five things that I did right that day. My successes! What did I do that day that was a success?

My success list:

1. Kept the house clean
2. Didn't yell at the kids.
3. Showered
4. Read a book alone
5. Answered my emails

This list does not have to be a dream catcher. It doesn't have to be huge accomplishments. It just has to give you the boost you need to realize that life is not a struggle. This boost will carry you through the next day. You will begin to see the small accomplishments however unimportant they may seem to others. Remember, we are not measuring ourselves up to someone else. We are looking only at ourselves. Be careful not to compare yourself to anyone. It won't work. Find what is important in your life. You will find that you will be happier with yourself. You will be brighter and see more light in your life. In the last chapter I spoke of the Path to Light and Love. This will help you to get on that path. It will help open you up to be viewed by yourself. So many of us live our lives with these ideas about ourselves. I think its called denial. We very often falsely build ourselves up. I say falsely because it is not easy to look at ones self honestly. When you write your list, (again it's all about the writing) you see on paper what you really are thinking your life is about.

Using the principles of this system, your life will change. Take a chance on yourself and practice the exercises described. If it's all too much for you, then take one principle and try that. You can do whatever you put your mind to. You've heard this all of your life and now it's time to start believing. We have more power than anyone we realize and once you tap into it you will change.

Printed in the United States
61031LVS00003B/151-159

9 781424 145560